The Rainbow Series of
To Touch The

G000095951

RAINBOW OF LOVE

Rainbow of Love

Book Three

Poetry by Chrissy Greenslade.
Illustrations by Niccola Ambrose.

PETRA PUBLISHING

RAINBOW OF LOVE

Copyright © Chrissy Greenslade. 2001

ISBN: 0-9534319-2-4

First Edition published Spring 2001 by
PETRA PUBLISHING
4, Leven Close
Bournemouth
BH4 9LP

" I dedicate this book
To the memory of my beloved Mom and Dad,
Annie and Sidney Reynolds,
And to all caring parents everywhere. "

Also by Chrissy Greenslade:
Book One - Rainbow of Life
Book Two - Rainbow of The Heart

British Library Cataloguing in Publication Data:
A catalogue record for this book is available from the British Library

Printed in China through World Print Ltd.

Layout & Design Mark A Fudge
design@fudgie.co.uk / www.fudgie.co.uk

CONTENTS

A Glimpse Of Heaven 9

Trolley Battle 10

Solace 11

Buttercup Game 12

An Angel For You 13

Cheers For Tears 14

A Walk In The Park 15

Brace Yourself 16

Diana's Way 17

There's Always One 18

Easter Message 19

I Don't Believe It 20

A Jay On The Lawn 21

A Sunny Day Is Forecast 22

I Can Only Try 24

The Tooth Fairy 25

Tribute To Dearest Mom 26

The Boutique 27

The Reprieve 28

Good Intentions 29

Turn To God And Pray 30

Patience is a virtue 31

A Blackbird's Release 32

Forty Winks 33

The Star .34

Household Blues 36

Knock On The Door 37

Autumn .38

Ode To Outfits 39

Sunset Promise 40

Oh, How I Would
Love A Good Read 41

Look For The Light 42

Testing Time 43

A Perfect Pair 44

Christmas Preparations 45

Bird's Breakfast 46

Magnification 48

Calamity .50

The Railway Cat 51

On Losing Your Husband 52

Hidden Longing 53

Woods 54

Freedom .55

Recycled Teenagers 56

Never Give Up 57

The Haven 58

Blessed Are The Hungry 59

Possessions 60

Discoveries 61

Christmas Angels 62

ACKNOWLEDGEMENTS

The following poems of mine have previously been published in the following magazines and annuals.

Dorset Anthology of Poems
(Lewis Manning Hospice)
Dorset
Diana's Way
The Reprieve.

The People's Friend
The Tooth Fairy

The Fireside Book
There's Always One
Breakfast in Bed
Serenade to Squirrels
Spring Cleaning

The Journal (DHWSHA)
Tribute to Dearest Mom.
Turn to God and Pray.

The Friendship Book
Trolley Battle.

The People's Friend Annual
Ode To Outfits.

The Lady
Woods.

New Vision
Magnification

Chrissy Greenslade thanks all her readers,
who sent such wonderful letters.
If you wish to be informed of forthcoming books in
the Rainbow Series please let her know at:

Petra Publishing,
4, Leven Close,
Bournemouth,
BH4 9PL
Telephone: 01202 762730
E-mail: chrissy@petrapublishing.co.uk   www.petrapublishing.co.uk

INTRODUCTION

Following the wonderful response from readers of my first two books, 'Rainbow of Life, and 'Rainbow of The Heart,' it is with much pleasure that I bring you the third book of my Rainbow Gift Book Series, 'Rainbow of Love.'

I have been so moved by your letters that I have included a few excerpts from them in the back of this book. I am really sorry that I cannot include more. I am so glad that the love, laughter, faith and comfort in my books has touched and helped you and hopefully added something special to your life. I know that once again you will be able to identify with many of my poems, which are based on life in all its rainbow colours.

I am non- profit making, but with God's and your support **I know** that I will reach my goal and complete my series of seven books. It is a mammoth task but 'All things are possible.' As there are seven colours of the rainbow, I intend there to be seven books, each with a cover representing a different colour of the rainbow. My fourth book 'Rainbow Magic,' is already in the process of being written.

Look for the poems in my book that are especially meaningful for **you**. Share my life and feelings and take my hand. With hope and joy in your heart, once again, cross over the rainbow with me.

Love and Light, Chrissy

For further information, book requirements, poetry readings and talks please contact
Chrissy Greenslade, Petra Publishing, 4 Leven Close, Bournemouth BH4 9LP
Tel: 01202 762730   E-mail address: chrissy@petrapublishing.co.uk
Internet website address: http://www.petrapublishing.co.uk

A GLIMPSE OF HEAVEN

There's a carpet of gold in the garden,
Golden rain falling down from the trees,
Which now flutter confetti of Autumn,
As their branches are swayed by the breeze.

It is said that the pathways of heaven,
Are all shining for they're paved with gold,
Then I know I've found heaven in my garden,
On this day as the summer grows old.

For the fir trees have beech decorations,
And the birdbath leaf islands that gleam,
The acacia clothed in its glory,
Is ablaze with red gems like a dream.

The huge maple next door is displaying,
Its leaves, yellowy green, still attached,
And the mulberry tint of the cherry,
On this canvas is perfectly matched.

Scarlet berries of holly are cheerful,
They're reminding me not to feel sad,
As I sweep up this beautiful carpet,
I remember the pleasure I've had.

TROLLEY BATTLE

Today I chose a different store,
My trolley overflowing,
But had to fight a battle,
To control where I was going.

For I had popped the coin into
A trolley that was truly,
The most annoying one to wield,
Its steering so unruly.

I tried to push it straight ahead,
But to the right it's veering,
And though I pull it to the left,
It ignores manual steering.

So having knocked into a shelf,
Soon tired, my hair I'm tearing,
And I decide I've had enough,
I must regain my bearing.

I drag the trolley from the front,
The handle I'm ignoring,
But still it goes from side to side,
My efforts still it 's flooring.

So I'll choose trolleys I can find,
Unlinked, then give a test run,
This store I'll choose, then who's in charge,
There won't be any question!

SOLACE

When a problem's too much,
And it's hurting your soul,
When you feel there is nowhere to turn,
You must seek for the light,
And hand over to God,
Then you'll soon find the comfort you yearn.

When you release your tears,
Share your doubts and your fears,
Then an answer will soon come to you,
Just hold on, don't give in,
And your peace you will win,
For God's there and He'll help pull you through.

BUTTERCUP GAME

Oh how I remember, though memories fade,
The game that we children in summer all played,
When meadows were scattered with buttercup gold,
We asked the same questions that our mothers told.

"Do you like butter or do you like cheese?"
She held up a buttercup, knelt on her knees,
So serious, intent then she gazed at my skin,
Her chubby hand trembling held under my chin.

"Oh Nan, how the yellow glows just like a light,
It really is magic," she cried with delight.
I smiled and decided that the truth could wait,
For all kinds of dairy food I really hate!

AN ANGEL FOR YOU

There's an angel for you and an angel for me,
For angels are everywhere, though we don't see,
And although our vision is clouded with doubt,
There are myriads and myriads of angels about.

They are there with the people who stand in the queue,
Who give up their seats on the buses for you,
They'll carry your shopping when you are in pain,
So look out for your angels, they'll be there again.

For an angel is present in friends who are kind,
An angel can touch you when troubled in mind,
A chat with your angel will ease your despair,
So be comforted, someone who loves you is there.

You are never alone for they come in disguise,
But they are real angels whatever their size,
They don't need great wings, though these too can appear,
If for you that's your angel, the one you hold dear.

But some angels are feelings, a form, shape or light,
For many you sense but aren't meant for your sight,
God's angels protect you, arrive on the scene,
Just at that precise moment where despair has been.

Also strangers are often an angel God sent,
To stop something happening, a mishap prevent,
They surround, enfold you when you are asleep,
And if you're feeling lonely, your vigil they keep.

Now when you're sad and down turn your face to the light,
And know that your angel's aware of your plight,
How cared for and calm now that you understand,
There is always your angel - just hold out your hand!

CHEERS FOR TEARS

He came and found me crying,
Concerned he looked at me,
"Whatever is the matter?"
I smiled back tearfully.

"I've poured through our old photos,
They make me feel so glad,
So thankful for the blessings,
And good life that we've had."

He kissed my cheek, now smiling,
Relieved he pressed my hand,
He knew female emotions,
Were hard to understand.

I really love a wedding,
But 'though I try to smile,
My tears unbidden gather,
As brides walk down the aisle.

My friend and I watch often,
A film, heart-rending, sad,
Both weeping, we enjoy it.
- To men, it must seem mad.

It's certainly amazing,
I wish that I knew why,
I always feel much better,
For having a good cry!

A WALK IN THE PARK

In the park the buds are plumping,
Secret shoots reveal their heads,
Seeking nuts with optimism,
Squirrels burrow in flower beds.

Early blossom holds a promise,
Shyly shaking out her dress,
Daffodils en masse and swaying,
Fill the park with cheerfulness.

Walkers welcome mellow sunshine,
Weeping willows spring awaits,
Children race, enjoy their freedom,
Play on swings and roller skates.

Dogs attended by their owners,
Strain at leashes to be free,
On the benches, reading, eating,
People chatter happily.

Sweet the air of parkland playtime,
Beauty, leisure time is free,
Hand in hand we smile, contented,
In the park where you took me.

BRACE YOURSELF

"I've lost ten pounds," he boasted,
He really did look trim,
I liked to see him slimmer,
I was so pleased for him.

Because he had been poorly,
His appetite was less,
And he was off his chocolate,
Which helped me I confess.

But what we weren't prepared for,
When chatting happily,
Was that his now loose trousers,
Would fall below his knee.

There was a whispered giggle,
Then laughter all around,
But oh I'm very grateful,
They'd not fallen to the ground!

DIANA'S WAY

We all of us know that
We want to be good,
To think the right things
And do all that we should,
But life is a challenge,
Has twists, it has turns,
Each way has a lesson,
And from it one learns.

As Diana tried,
So has Diana cried,
She's had to face critics,
Fight anger and pride,
She wanted to love,
And she wanted to serve,
In front of the world,
It took courage and nerve.

We all need a time,
When we must be alone,
A time to face God,
To seek help, to atone,
But sensitive people
Need help to be strong,
Need guidance, direction,
So they won't go wrong.

God knows how she tried,
How she lived, how she died,
The impact she made,
Is the love we can't hide,
Imagine the stresses,
That had to be faced,
Don't step out of line,
Or you're chased or disgraced.

They lived and they laughed,
Seeking refuge they died,
But the man that she loved,
Was at least by her side,
Together they both
Have found eternal peace,
Where their wordly problems
And troubles will cease.

So lighten your heart,
For they walk hand in hand,
She'll always send guidance,
Her boys understand;
She'll live in their heart,
Once they've settled and grieved,
For in Diana's short life-time,
God's way she achieved.

THERE'S ALWAYS ONE

He kept his eye upon her
And sighed, it was still there,
Her coffee cup was brimming,
It really wasn't fair!

Collecting all the empties,
He cast a beady eye
Upon her - she was chatting,
He had to pass her by.

Ah, good, she'd started drinking,
Oh no, she'd stopped again,
These thoughtless, chatty ladies,
They really were a pain.

She's laughing, says she's sorry,
She's drinking it now fast,
He smiled, for now the tables
Were completely cleared at last!

EASTER MESSAGE

There's a stirring on earth,
Now that Easter is here,
There is laughter and loving and hope,
There's a firm reassurance,
Everything will be well,
That with challenges, problems we'll cope.

It's a time of renewal,
And a time of rebirth,
For the flowers, for the trees, for the world,
When we all share the joy,
That is filling our heart,
Then the love in the world is unfurled.

So let's all now rejoice,
Fill the world with the truth,
Let our light shine for us and each other,
Then in one great accord,
Just like Jesus our Lord,
We'll share peace, light and love, with our brother.

I DON'T BELIEVE IT!

I can't take him anywhere,
It really is a pain,
Oh what a fuss that he has caused,
He's done it once again.

They are not in the bedroom,
They are not in the bar,
Or on the breakfast table, but
They really can't be far.

The management is searching,
The room-maids too and friends,
We've bought some bars of chocolate,
So we can make amends.

You never will believe it,
They're in his other jacket,
I wish now I'd brought only one,
That I'd forgot to pack it.

So now I keep an eye on him,
Just everywhere he passes,
Or once again I'll hear him say,
"Oh dear I've lost my glasses!"

A JAY ON THE LAWN

There's a jay on the lawn,
Look, a jay, oh a jay,
On this beautiful morning,
This first day in May.

Holding fast to my breath,
As I kept statue-still,
Fascinated I stood by
My lounge window-sill.

Then it shyly explored
Titbits scattered around,
It's proud beak on display
As it pecked on the ground.

With a quick, nervous glance,
Oh, it flew, oh it flew,
Flashing beautiful colours
Of pink, white and blue.

Such a colourful bird,
How I laughed at the note,
Which then suddenly came
With a 'craak' from its throat.

God had made it that way,
And now God made my day,
On the lawn I had seen,
For the first time a jay.

A SUNNY DAY IS FORECAST

The topsy-turvey weather
Is upsetting all the town,
The plans which all the town folk made,
Have been turned upside down.

At No. One old Mr. Brown was working in his garden,
And Mr. Young at No. Two hoped his cement would harden.
At No. Three the washing blew and flapped up in the sky,
And Mrs. Green was quite serene for it would soon be dry.

At No. Four the clothes he wore were made for warmth and sun,
As Tommy was on holiday he thought he'd have some fun.
At No. Five the barbecue was lit and coals were hot,
And people laughed and chatted and their daily cares forgot.

At No. Six on step-ladder Molly her windows sloshed
With water, then she polished them, till all was bright and washed.
Len cleaned his car at No. Seven and took out the front seat,
Beth sunbathing at No. Eight was lapping up the heat.

Her sister Kathleen mowed the lawn and outside No. Nine,
Pete's mother sat and mended, sipping at her home-made wine.
At No. Ten in curtained shade, Grandad enjoyed T.V.
The sun too hot he watched the cricket with a cup of tea.

Then suddenly down came the rain, Mr. Brown rushed to his shed,
And Mr. Young, his cement wet, was angry and bright red.
Poor Mrs. Green, her washing wet - not raining now but hailing,
Was heard as far as No. Ten, both grumbling and bewailing.

Young Tommy's shorts were stuck to him, the barbecue a mess,
And Molly's windows streaked with rain and dust, as you can guess.
So sodden were the car covers, Len had to wring them out,
And as the rain fell on her skin, Kath's sister gave a shout.

The lawn-mower was rushed inside, jeans could be patched again,
And Grandad fumed because they said, 'Play stopped, because of rain.'
Then as the street resigned itself to work inside that day,
The sun returning to the sky, laughed rain clouds clear away.

Then doubtfully heads peeped outside to see what had got wet,
They all came out bewildered, shaking heads, their day upset.
Although the storm had almost brought them to the end of their tether,
They bravely smiled, then blamed the ones who'd forecast sunny weather!

I CAN ONLY TRY

Oh how much I would like to be perfect,
But no matter how hard that I try,
There are times when frustrations and problems,
Cause reactions I'd like to deny.

I don't mean to be bad or be hurtful,
When responses are not what they ought,
It is then I feel guilty and sorry,
Just because of a thoughtless retort.

But God knows of my struggles and pressures,
He's aware that I try to be good,
And I'm sure that the next time I need Him,
He will help me react as I should.

So though it would be nice to be perfect,
I must not make my aims quite so high,
For I know I am making some progress,
I'm still learning to walk, not to fly.

So I'm asking that God will be patient,
When sometimes things just never go right,
For I know He loves me, that I'm His child,
And I'm perfect enough in His sight.

THE TOOTH FAIRY

My tooth is loose and wobbly,
It makes me feel all funny,
I keep on pushing with my tongue,
To make more pocket money.

You see there is a fairy,
Who's very keen on teeth,
She creeps beneath my pillow when
My tooth is underneath.

It must be very heavy,
The fifty that she brings,
But probably it helps a lot,
That fairies have strong wings.

I never hear her coming,
Although I stay awake,
I never feel her searching for
The tooth she has to take.

I wonder if she's using
My teeth as fairy bricks,
To build herself a little house,
With magic fairy tricks?

Now as I'm six next birthday,
Maybe she'll realise,
I'm big now and she will leave me,
A pound as a surprise!

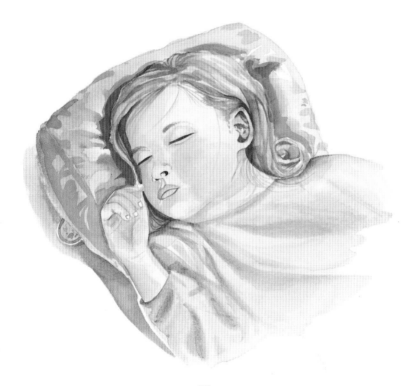

TRIBUTE TO DEAREST MOM

Beloved mother, there was no other,
Who was so kind and good,
You lived your life and gave your love,
As every mother should.

God gave you me and gave me you,
I chose you for my own,
And lessons that I've learnt from you,
I've cherished as I've grown.

You made our childhood happy
With your gentle, loving care,
You gave us comfort, dried our tears,
For you were always there.

Your days were not exciting for
You gave us all your life,
You cooked for us, looked after us,
Our mother and a wife.

But you are very special
And when you have had a rest,
Your new life will be full of joy,
For you deserve the best.

You were so full of courage and
So brave these past few years,
And how you tried to smile for us,
When we were full of tears.

We are relieved that you are now
Released from grief and pain,
Oh little Mommy we're so glad
That you are whole again.

How hard it was to leave us all,
For you still loved us so,
You didn't want to see us cry,
But had to let life go.

And we're not sad, because you're free
For your new life has started,
And we are closer on this day,
We never can be parted.

How wonderful you must have felt,
As all your loved ones met you,
Oh dearest Mom we love you so,
We never will forget you.

For you are in our hearts, our lives,
Which you nurtured and tended,
And now your body's as God made,
Youthful and healed and mended.

I know you're in the summerlands,
With beauty all around you,
And that the truth that life goes on,
Will probably astound you.

But just like me you had your faith,
And you're where you belong,
Oh Mom you're where life's wonderful,
In heaven you're well and strong.

So if we shed a tear sometimes,
And in our heart feel pain,
We'll let it go and think with joy,
Of the day we'll meet again.

THE BOUTIQUE

Evening dresses stood tall in the window,
Their sheer elegance caused me to gasp,
For they glistened and shimmered so slinky,
Some stole-draped held by brooch or a clasp.

How I gazed at a gown, oh so splendid,
It was streamlined to such a degree,
That I 'oohed' and I 'ahhed,' as I stood there,
I was totally weak at the knee.

So I entered enthusing and pointing
At silk dresses all fit for a queen,
Some were sexy and satin or flimsy,
The most gorgeous that I'd ever seen.

The decision to choose the ideal one,
The modele that I'd die to possess,
Was affected of course by the price tag,
Hung discreetly on each superb dress.

As I couldn't decide, make my mind up,
I drank coffee then knew what to do,
For the dress which I'd loved
  in a Charity shop,
Cost not two hundred pounds,
  but just two!

THE REPRIEVE

In the woods there's a rustling,
A trembling suspense,
A restlessness stirred in the breeze,
There's a creaking of branches,
An ominous hush,
With a whirr of wings birds leave
The trees.

They could hear the machine
With its hideous noise,
Get closer and closer to them,
With a sigh and a shiver,
They heard their friends die,
As they whispered a shaky
'Amen.'

From its momentous height
Now the oldest beech gazed
At massacred trees down below,
As it spread out its branches,
And breathed love around,
It encouraged new seedlings
To grow.

Then as more trees were felled
And more beauty dispelled,
A sadness crept into the night,
Lucky trees who remained,
Turned their branches to God,
And felt blessings of warmth, love
And light.

When the morning arrived,
A new courage they found,
To face the machine and their fate,
But a triumphant crowd
Raced with papers in hand,
Shouting, "Thank God, it's still not
Too late!"

As the dreaded machines
Were then driven away,
Remaining trees breathed with relief,
And excitement returned
With the insects and birds,
As the wood filled with hope now,
Not grief.

Many foresters cheered
With the group that stood there,
To protest was all that was needed,
And God smiled at the trees
Who had asked for His help,
For good thoughts and good men
Had succeeded!

GOOD INTENTIONS

Do big stores and supermarkets
Have a bad effect on you,
And change your good intentions,
Just to spend a pound or two?

Now I needed only three things,
Cereal, a cake, some tea,
But then I saw some bargains,
Spread on shelves attracting me.

For that day I'd fetched my pension,
So I knew I'd pay my way,
But all my good intentions,
They just simply slipped away.

There were lots of special offers,
Some half-price or get one free,
Bargains and free containers,
That were luring, tempting me.

Now I've always hated shopping,
Though my loved one finds it fun,
But now I am the person,
Who buys two instead of one.

I am told that any freezer,
Runs much cheaper when it's full,
And if I have the money,
Choosing things is never dull

I am not a shopaholic,
What's this ditty all about?
I went in to buy three things,
And had twelve when I came out!

TURN TO GOD AND PRAY

Whenever things seem upside down,
And God seems far away,
Your Father's there to share your stress,
So turn to Him and pray.

For prayer is just a way to talk
To God your closest Friend,
Someone to tell your secrets to,
Someone you won't offend.

For God is love and you are love,
His spark is in us all,
And if you turn to Him you'll find.
He'll catch you when you fall.

He'll ease your pain and heal your heart,
He'll show you how to live,
And if you listen carefully,
His guidance He will give.

His still, small voice you soon can hear,
Don't doubt the words He'll say,
For in your thoughts He'll send His word,
If you turn to Him and pray.

PATIENCE IS A VIRTUE

I'm sitting in the car park,
Our ticket's overdue,
You said you'd be a short time,
Where you are I have no clue.

I can't go now and find you,
I don't know where to look,
I'll try to keep good tempered,
So I'll start my library book.

The shoppers are returning
With goodies to their car,
Oh, it is getting dark now,
And I'm wondering where you are.

That man looks like a warden,
He is! Oh no he's not.
This really is nerve wracking,
You have put me in a spot.

I'll take my purse and pretend,
I'm searching for my change,
You could turn up this minute,
Something soon I must arrange.

I can't stand this much longer,
I'll put more money in,
That's better! As I return,
I decide that I can't win.

For here you are approaching,
A smile upon your face,
I will keep cool, for what I feel,
Is really a disgrace!

A BLACK BIRD'S RELEASE

We found him near the roadside,
Where he'd dragged himself in pain,
For the car and speed had hit him,
Left him suffering in the rain.

Of course the tiny impact
Of a bird upon its wheel,
Wasn't anything the driver
Or the passengers could feel.

Perhaps one cried 'You've hit it'
And then didn't want to look,
But the fragile, little blackbird,
A great, deadly blow it took.

So bravely he had faced it,
With his useless leg askew,
As he struggled wings a flutter,
Aiming where long grasses grew.

And that is where I found him,
Sadly looking up at me,
And from there I gently took him
To that blessed sanctuary.

I rang the given number,
Where at once they welcomed him,
Lovingly they smiled and nursed him.
Though they knew his chance was slim.

They couldn't heal my blackbird,
Though in every way they tried,
And they even rang to tell me,
That my dear blackbird had died.

Although they couldn't save him,
In my heart I am not sad,
For I knew what love and caring,
All the tenderness he'd had.

So in his blackbird heaven,
As he flies now whole and free,
I know he sings his sweetest song,
For his carers and for me.

FORTY WINKS

The time is right for me tonight,
To sit beside the fire,
It's time to rest, I've done my best,
From work I'll now retire.

I've cooked a meal, cleaned a great deal,
My armchair looks inviting,
The fire's good, I've fetched the wood,
The tele. looks exciting.

The sound of rain on window pane,
Makes me feel warm and cosy,
I'm safe and dry, though winds are high,
My cheeks are feeling rosy.

The coffee's hot inside the pot,
My slippered feet are glowing,
I feel content, wood-perfumed scent,
My sleepiness is growing.

I've woken up, cold coffee cup,
I must soon stop this yawning;
The fire is dead, it's time for bed,
Or I won't get up in the morning.

THE STAR

The tramp lay on his back on a bench in the park,
It was bitterly cold, it was raining and dark,
He turned up his collar to keep out the cold,
He was starving and penniless, lonely, felt old.

Now despair was the victor, he lay back to die,
But then suddenly there it stood bright in the sky,
He blinked at the star, at the strength of its light,
It was then that he knew he'd not give up the fight.

For there must be a place, where he could lay his head,
He had searched till he dropped, but he would find a bed,
He gathered his kit and then spoke to the star,
"You found Mary a bed and brought kings from afar."

With one eye on the star and one eye on the road,
He then dragged his tired body to find his abode,
Some travellers passing called out, saw his plight,
"There's a shelter near here. You can stay for the night."

So he tagged on behind - water seeped through his shoe,
Sore and sodden his feet and his hands turning blue,
But he knew with comfort his star was still there,
It seemed bigger and brighter, spread light everywhere.

And believe it or not, it appeared that it stopped
As he fainted, collapsed. On the pavement he dropped.
His unshaven friends gathered round him, one went
To the door of the building which God's love had sent.

Then they lifted him up and they took him inside,
And when he had recovered with weakness he cried,
"My star brought me here, I knew that it would!"
In a clean bed and nightclothes, he felt warm, so good.

Kindly faces were smiling as they brought him tea,
Then he knew he'd found love, perhaps a new liberty,
It now was the time he should live snug and dry,
That was what his star meant that shone down from the sky.

It had led him to reason, he'd been in a state,
But he had found a haven, it wasn't too late.
When his dad had died, he'd let go, didn't think,
He'd got hooked on the drugs and he'd taken to drink.

Now he heard happy voices, some singing not sad,
Oh how could people laugh when their life was so bad?
A lady said, " Cheer up! Now you can believe,
That it really is Christmas. Tonight's Christmas Eve!

"When you're rested, eat up." So he took a huge bite,
His new friend said, "Then join in our carols tonight."
The first thing he saw on the huge Christmas tree,
Was a star, and he whispered "That star is for me."

Smiling eyes of the helpers, were tender and kind,
And he found that hope stirred, a new life he would find,
These people would help him to give up the dope,
Then he grinned at the star, for at last he had hope.

HOUSEHOLD BLUES

I was busy sorting washing,
When the phone began to ring,
So I finished in a hurry,
And I threw in everything.

Yet another wretched salesman.
Double glazing! I felt cross,
Irritated, put the powder in,
And watched the washing toss.

Well at least something was started,
But I was so much behind,
So I went upstairs to make the beds,
A poem on my mind.

Then I did my jobs as usual,
And scribbled words that came,
On the backs of envelopes and such,
- Housework! It was a shame,

That I couldn't wave a wand now,
And make everything all straight,
So that in my study I could go,
On writing concentrate.

All the washing should be dry now,
- Oh, there was so much to do!
But I stopped, rooted in horror,
For the clothes were a deep blue.

I soon saw the culprit lying,
A new hand-towel I had bought,
Those annoying, nuisance salesmen,
Oh, I daren't reveal my thought.

For I have a piebald sweater,
Which had once been a pure white,
And my nighty, blouse and cardigan
Are not a pretty sight.

But sometimes at first things can seem,
So much worse than you would think,
For what if my Love's underwear,
Had been a vivid pink!

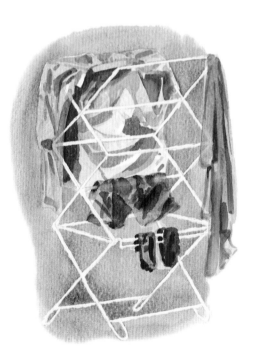

KNOCK ON THE DOOR

You've knocked on the door,
Now please open your heart,
And wait for the blessings
In your life to start.

Once the door is open,
Then just step inside,
You'll lose anger, sadness,
Frustration and pride.

God's love will astound you,
His power make you strong,
Then you will be guided,
And never go wrong.

The first step is taken,
So leave doubts behind,
Just search and keep searching,
Then God you will find.

AUTUMN

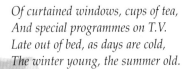

For many people autumn brings
Depression amongst other things,
For it's a time which can bring sighs,
When winter waits as summer dies.

But it is such a special time,
Of mellow fruit and mature wine,
A time of gentle garden chores,
Of coloured leaves,
* gold-brackened moors.*

As the last swallow flies away,
The haws and hips make
  hedgerows gay;
For creatures who need winter sleep,
It is a time to store and reap

Their harvest - and for me and you,
It's steaming soup and warming stew.
The earth and trees are glad to rest,
The hedgehog curls up in his nest.

We put our summer clothes away,
But still enjoy a sunny day,
And after limp and languid heat,
The nip of cold is crisp and sweet.

The swirl of leafy, bonfire smoke,
Our senses please, pictures provoke
Of roaring fires and buttered toast,
Those cosy times we love the most;

Of curtained windows, cups of tea,
And special programmes on T.V.
Late out of bed, as days are cold,
The winter young, the summer old.

Our outdoor work becoming less,
More time to read, relieved of stress.
Our letters can be answered too,
Because the daylight hours are few.

And when we're tired of being indoors,
Weary of sitting, doing chores,
Autumn then shares its
* greatest treasure,*
Paints red-gold landscapes for
* our pleasure.*

It brings us mild and balmy days,
And soothes us with its winning ways,
We crunch the leaves beneath our feet,
Smile at the people whom we meet.

Autumn arrives for many reasons,
So be grateful for our change
* of seasons,*
With optimism hope will grow,
As we welcome autumn and
* let summer go.*

ODE TO OUTFITS

There is something about a uniform,
Which I cannot quite define,
It's not so much the colour,
Or the cut or shape or line.

It's a kind of splendid grandeur,
It's a neatness, it's a kit,
It's a dashing, smart distinction,
With its undisputed fit.

There's a manliness that's striking,
A correctness and a pride,
Which can make a good impression,
And transforms the man inside.

How I love all national costumes,
Sturdy males dressed to the hilt,
But the one who makes my knees go weak,
Is the Scot who wears a kilt!

SUNSET PROMISE

Our day had been a special one,
A feast of winter treats,
Bright sunshine had surprised us as
We explored cobbled streets.

Blue skies had warmed the ice-cold day,
And filled us with elation,
We'd wandered down the country lanes,
Enjoying God's creation.

The village church still bore the marks,
Where ancient feet had trod,
Mosaic windows streamed with light,
Giving a sense of God.

How could we leave it all behind?
Too soon the day had ended,
But as the sun began to set,
Our spirits soon transcended.

The sky became a wonderland,
Of gold, then pink, then red,
A heavenly world, mountains, a lake,
Were there above our head.

We held our breath, sated our eyes,
Watching each picture changing,
Cloud faces, birds, landscapes we saw,
Like magic rearranging.

The sun sank slowly behind hills,
Its blushes catching fire,
Chasing with flames, the fluffy clouds,
Highlighting a church spire.

Rays lit the land as we went home,
They painted trees, the road,
The sunset bathed our hearts with hope,
As peace within us flowed.

OH, HOW I WOULD LIKE A GOOD READ

I went to the library and chose
 a good book,
Deciding I'd have a good read,
But each time I tried,
I felt I could have cried,
For I somehow could never succeed.

At home I sat down with a nice cup of tea,
I picked up my book - oh what joy!
I put up my feet,
It was really a treat,
Till a shout came from my paper boy.

He'd made a mistake with the papers
 he'd brought,
Disturbed I went back to my book,
Then frantic I heard,
My cat chasing a bird,
So I knew I must go out and look.

The phone rang - I answered, - not
 very polite,
My book still unread once again,
A neighbour came 'round,
Disappointment I drowned,
Then it suddenly started to rain.

Frustrated I rushed for my washing,
 now damp,
I folded, then put it away,
I looked at the time,
It was really a crime,
Where on earth had the hours gone today?

The children came home, there were
 meals then to get,
No reading till they were in bed,
My other half snored,
With the book I adored,
I dropped off - so it still wasn't read.

As sadly I gave up my 'good read' to sleep,
I quickly got rid of my sorrow,
I've made up my mind,
I shall definitely find,
Extra time for my reading tomorrow..

LOOK FOR THE LIGHT

Now is the time when you've given up the fight,
And your world seems to be inside out,
To ask in your prayer, for the strength you'll find there,
Then you'll know what your problem's about.

Still filled with pain, feeling there is no hope,
When the future appears black and bleak,
Do not give up hope, you will find you can cope,
You'll discover the purpose you seek.

Behind the dark clouds there's a sky blue and clear,
And a bright, rainbow promise not far,
Just choose then your fate, for it's never too late,
Start again now you know where you are.

Throughout your sorrow, you will find tomorrow,
God will open new doors free of strife,
I know then you'll find, in this fresh state of mind,
Once again joy and peace in your life.

TESTING TIME

My friend glowing with virtue
Said "I've lost a lot of weight,
I've lived on salads, yoghurt, fruit,
And all the things I hate.

I've given up jam doughnuts,
And the butter I scrape thin,
For I am quite determined,
That this battle I shall win."

I admired all her efforts,
Was so glad for her own sake,
But I could see her weaken
When she saw the coffee cake.

I watched with great amusement,
As her eyes devoured the slice,
She licked her lips, then looked away,
Then sighed. It was so nice!

It really shouldn't matter
What big difference could it make?
Just once a small piece - well not huge-
Of creamy, gooey cake.

Her taste buds won the battle
As she grinned and said, "That one!"
And from that moment, thrust aside,
Her diet plans had gone!

A PERFECT PAIR

Today you have made a commitment,
You are married, you're now man and wife,
And your love that has made this decision,
Will grow stronger the rest of your life.

It is not just the magic of knowing,
You have found someone close who will care
Whether you are unhappy or happy,
It's just great knowing someone is there.

At the times when you need reassuring,
When the things in life don't go quite right,
It's that wonderful, comfortable feeling,
That your other half's holding you tight.

For to care and to share is the purpose,
Then the knot you have tied will not bind,
But bring laughter and joy not restriction,
And soon peace of mind too you will find

For today's just a symbol, a gesture,
To ask God to bless your brand new start,
So we send bride and groom our best wishes,
And of course, all our love from the heart.

CHRISTMAS PREPARATIONS

I said I would start early,
Make sure that I had time,
To buy my gifts at leisure,
For rushing is a crime.
But Christmas has come early,
Or so it seems to me,
For I have only three weeks,
Not long you must agree.

I haven't bought my cards yet,
Although I've made a list,
My parcels for abroad now,
Should go or they'll be missed.
I've brought my wrapping paper,
At least, 1'm glad to say,
But I must buy some presents,
To wrap without delay.

My list of cards looks longer,
The price to post, oh, dear!
I'm feeling panic rising,
As Christmas day draws near.
But now I have decided,
To stop and think it out,
Of course I will be ready,
Of that there is no doubt.

For I remember last year,
I fussed, worried and flapped,
And yet I was in good time,
Prepared, delivered, wrapped.
So calmly I've decided,
To write my cards tonight,
And wrap the distant parcels,
That definitely seems right,

If cards are late arriving,
The post could be to blame,
Letters I'll write at New Year,
- It always is the same!
I'm going to make an effort,
To take it nice and steady,
But my New Year's Resolution is
Next Autumn I'll be ready!

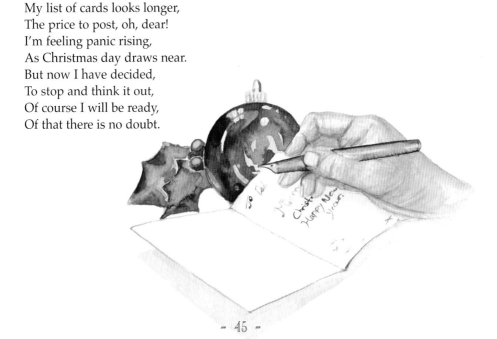

BIRD'S BREAKFAST

A whistling wind howls round the house,
Sleet lashes bent and barren trees,
As icy winner does its best,
The lakes, the moor and ponds to freeze.

Snow flakes now falling fast and free,
Are dancing madly all around,
And like a magnet drawing me,
I watch them carpet hedge and ground.

Their magic lures me as I see
The world washed clean, transformed in white,
My nose pressed to the window-pane,
I'm lost in wonder at the sight.

Within the hour I warmly dress,
And venture to that virgin land,
I leave my foot-prints on the lawn,
The dish now empty in my hand.

The cold snaps at my cheeks and nose,
As hastily I race inside,
For snow-scenes I appreciate,
Far more from my warm fire-side.

How glad I am as down they swoop,
Their 'arrow heads' left in a row,
As eagerly my feathered friends,
Retrieve their breakfast from the snow.

Content, I hear the kettle sing,
As flickering flames, armchair invite,
I know I've helped them to survive,
I smile as they fly out or sight.

MAGNIFICATION

What appears as a speck can become very big,
If it's linked to the power of The Source,
As a phrase chosen well, which is wise and profound,
May result in a worthwhile discourse.

For from miniature seeds massive forests can grow,
So for us that's what each effort's for,
For in harmony it's the example we show,
In our lives, lived in peace, not by war.

When a few drops of water turn into rainfall,
It helps crops, trees and plants to survive,
As communion with God in our thoughts and our prayers,
Will our hope and our love keep alive.

For our Father sees clearly His spark in us all,
This can suddenly burst into flame,
Which will burn very brightly, spread light throughout life,
If it shines with His love, in His name.

Oh how small and inadequate we feel we are,
Until seen under God's microscope,
There our efforts enlarge like a gigantic star,
And bring goodness and thoughts full of hope.

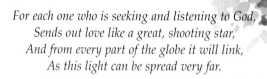

For each one who is seeking and listening to God,
Sends out love like a great, shooting star,
And from every part of the globe it will link,
As this light can be spread very far.

For when each little group gathers here on the earth,
And God's radiance is touching our meetings,
All the Elders rejoice and are filled with new hope,
At our simplicity and our greetings.

Then the angels all laugh as they gather our prayers,
And the trusting love sent from below,
As they sprinkle this stardust, the truth, all around,
How they smile as the earth starts to glow.

Then our sincere groups linked themselves with God's light,
Are amazed at the peace in their heart,
And a purpose, a meaning, a oneness is felt,
From this moment they're given a new start.

So no matter how tiny we feel that we are,
Unimportant our lives always seem,
Every good, loving thought is the power that we need,
To achieve the impossible dream.

CALAMITY

The freezer has defrosted,
For dishes I am looking,
It is just like a restaurant,
With all this food I'm cooking

The sausage rolls smell super,
The turkey steaks are browning,
But when we'll eat up this ice cream,
Is the reason why I'm frowning.

I've gobbled up a dishful,
For I hate being wasteful
But now I've nibbled this and that,
I'm full, it was so tasteful.

Chicken we'll have on Monday,
And fish we'll have for dinner,
A gateaux and a trifle - help!
- If only I was thinner.

We have to eat the liver,
The garlic bread and curries,
There is so much that's cooked now,
I haven't any worries.

Now I've phoned the repair man,
My calmness I'm regaining,
I'll fetch my washing as its dry,
Oh no, it's started raining!

THE RAILWAY CAT

He'd wake and stretch at once alert,
For breakfast brought anticipation,
Then warm and filled with love and food,
He'd set off for the railway station.

The steps he mounted swift and sure,
Looking around in expectation,
From clerk and passengers there came
A greeting at the railway station.

He loved the place, its crannies, nooks,
The noise of trains, a grand sensation,
His friends and titbits, comfy chair,
That Benji had at Weymouth Station.

One day he'd jumped on to a train,
For suddenly he'd felt temptation,
And full of glee as backs were turned,
He took a trip from Weymouth station.

They'd searched for him with
    apprehension,
Brought him back home with great
    elation,
For Benji had become a part
Of British Rail at his train Station.

When Benji died his friends were
    saddened,
Their cat was in a new dimension,
But comforted, they knew he'd find,
His heaven resembled Weymouth station.

ON LOSING YOUR HUSBAND

I hope I'll reassure you that
Your husband's very near,
He knows just how you're feeling,
As you brush away a tear.

For now he starts his great, new life,
The same but well and stronger,
Discarding his old 'overcoat, '
Not needed any longer.

He didn't want to leave you here,
Alone, sad and afraid,
But knew that things would soon get worse,
If longer he had stayed.

So please be full of comfort that
Your Love is whole again,
He's missing you and loves you too,
But glad to have no pain.

His new life's just beginning with
His loved ones and old friends,
It's all so very beautiful,
Where summer never ends.

Although you cannot see him,
He is very close to you,
He tries to cheer you when you're down,
And guide the things you do,

You both need time for grieving,
For you'll miss each other's touch,
And contact's so important,
When you love so very much.

But soon you'll find you will not want,
To hold him back with tears,
So gently you will free him and
Grow stronger with the years.

He'll understand the progress that
He made throughout his life,
But always when you need him,
He'll be there for you, his wife.

He'll help you from the other side,
His love it will not die,
He'll stroke your hair when you're asleep,
Dry your tears when you cry.

Our prayers for love and healing soon
Will help you through your grief,
Be sure in time God's strength and love,
Will bring peace and relief.

HIDDEN LONGING

My friend revealed a secret,
A yearning that he'd had,
And as it's in the open now,
He's feeling really glad.

There was a special item,
To aid him, make him smart,
But he'd had such a problem,
This longing to impart.

So delicate a subject,
But serious request,
And if his son would order it,
This gift would be the best

So plucking up his courage,
He asked his son-in-law,
And all the titters, silently,
Courageously he bore

I'd like this, a hair trimmer!
He took a nonchalant pose,
No not a trimmer for his head,
But the hairs inside his nose!

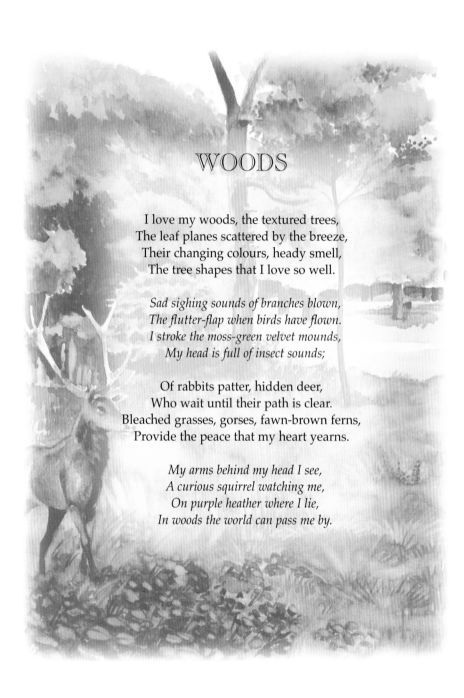

WOODS

I love my woods, the textured trees,
The leaf planes scattered by the breeze,
Their changing colours, heady smell,
The tree shapes that I love so well.

Sad sighing sounds of branches blown,
The flutter-flap when birds have flown.
I stroke the moss-green velvet mounds,
My head is full of insect sounds;

Of rabbits patter, hidden deer,
Who wait until their path is clear.
Bleached grasses, gorses, fawn-brown ferns,
Provide the peace that my heart yearns.

My arms behind my head I see,
A curious squirrel watching me,
On purple heather where I lie,
In woods the world can pass me by.

FREEDOM

He stood beside the willow near the stream,
A little boy lost in his childhood dream,
He gazed into the jar he held with awe,
Delighted with the minnows that he saw.

Then tousle-haired, his freckle face alight,
-His rolled up trousers feeling rather tight,
He gently dipped his net and let it lie,
Until more silvery friends came swimming by.

With care he tipped his captives from the net,
Then sat and watched their actions as he ate.
His jar in view he lay amongst the flowers,
His red, bare feet hinted at many hours

He'd trod where tickling weeds on stony bed,
His brave family of minnows hid and fed.
He knew they couldn't in his jar remain,
His hearty was torn! He let them go again.

For freedom was their life, it was his joy,
And they must both retain it, fish and boy.
So kneeling on the bank he said goodbye,
But mingled with the splash, I heard a sigh.

RECYCLED TEENAGERS

We're not old, just recycled teenagers,
Grey-haired, young man and elderly girl,
We're as necessary to creation,
As an oyster shell is to a pearl.

For inside we are dashing and longing
To do just as we did in our youth,
But we all get more tired and more achey,
So admit it and do tell the truth.

Yet our feet can't keep still when there's music,
For we love the quick-step and the waltz,
And if people think we are all past it,
Their impressions are completely false.

We love singing old songs with great gusto,
Playing Bingo we win the first line,
So although on the outside we're 'Oldies,'
Our teenager souls not in decline.

Although some may need sticks to aid walking,
Doing crosswords we have a quick mind,
And so many recycled teenagers,
Have more laughter and humour you'll find.

Yes we do like our comfort and cat-nap,
But when we've had our afternoon rest,
We will show you the way to enjoy life,
Oh, recycled teenagers are best!

NEVER GIVE UP

Do you ever despair of your face,
Intended for beauty and grace?
When I look at the lines,
Which ageing defines,
I feel it's a total disgrace.

Then I pick up the powder and paint,
And hide what is there with restraint,
As I darken my eyes,
See the made-up disguise,
The sight there would startle a saint.

No the answer is not found this way,
I must keep those frown lines at bay,
If the lines round my eyes,
Bring forth laughter not sighs,
Perhaps I'll look youthful and gay.

With a splash of clean water and soap,
And a dash of that fledgling called hope,
Brush my hair till it shines,
Call them my laughter lines,
I've decided with age I can cope.

THE HAVEN

They arrive on her doorstep, wings broken and lame,
Some are dumped in a ditch, tied in sacks for a game,
They've been tortured, neglected, maltreated, unfed,
Some were cared for so badly, they should have been dead.

There are cats, sad-eyed dogs, a tame tortoise or two,
Donkeys, horses and parrots to name but a few,
They're the battered, the saddened, the damaged, the old,
All subjected to misery, left out in the cold

But the little old lady from Nettlebridge Lane,
She will come to their rescue again and again,
Though the fund's running low and her home overflows,
She's still counting her blessings as her family grows.

For the moment they enter her haven of peace,
Their sad, pitiful crying and fearfulness cease,
Then they fill out and flourish, security find,
With this loving old lady, so gentle and kind.

She's a bent white-haired angel in wellies and coat,
She is often attended by Billy the goat,
There is sometimes a rabbit or hen at her feet,
And a glimpse of her fox cub's a rare, special treat.

But today there's a problem, a lot on her mind,
For a speedy solution she somehow must find,
There is quite a dilemma in Nettlebridge Lane,
For a monkey's arriving at ten on the train!

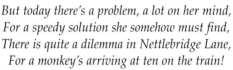

BLESSED ARE THE HUNGRY

Oh, how can a child feel it's blessed when its hungry?
And how can it cope with the pain and the fear?
How do we explain, it's a fact and not fiction,
That though there's no food that God's love is still here?

It needs all mankind to prevent all this suffering,
To make it the last time a child has to cry,
It needs an awareness of greedy intentions,
To channel the love so a child will not die.

The world if united could help all the starving,
To prevent their need, wealth and food would be spread,
But also uniting in prayer we are helping,
For love's powerful force is in prayers that are said.

But whilst mankind struggles to right all the wrong ways,
For us it's a comfort to know they are blessed,
For them there's a future in God's many mansions,
Where hunger's not known, only love, joy and rest.

POSSESSIONS

As I drew the curtains,
My ornament fell.
I just couldn't help it,
I let out a yell,
I felt cross and sad,
For I'd loved it so well;
But it's only a thing.

My favourite necklace
Got caught in my hair,
I struggled to free it,
It's really unfair,
I've broken the chain
Now it's needing repair;
But it's only a thing.

If sometimes unnoticed
Things get in the way,
Then break or are damaged,
I hide my dismay,
For they gave such pleasure,
Except for today,
And they are only things.

I've made up my mind,
I'll get rid of this clutter
For dusting takes time
And I grumble and mutter,
But passing a gift shop
My heart gives a flutter,
Oh what beautiful things!

I guiltily place it
In my cabinet,
And think that this sculpture's
The best I have yet,
My pleasure's so great,
I completely forget,
It is only a thing!

DISCOVERIES

She crouched engrossed in earnest glee,
Each chubby hand on dimpled knee;
She sniffed a flower to test its scent,
Observing where small insects went.

She noticed ants and woodlice pass,
As she lay face-down in the grass;
Then on her back she watched gulls soar,
Wondering what they were crying for.

Entranced she stroked smooth,
  satin stones,
Green, velvet moss and textured cones;
Her grubby hands explored moist soil,
Quite unaware of clothes she'd spoil.

Beneath the trees she found new birth,
Life stirring, shooting from the earth;
She pondered where the brown
  bulbs went,
Dug deep with fingers, lost, intent.

I smiled for I had been the same,
When I was young and life a game;
"Aunty," she called her face alight,
She ran to me, I held her tight.

My little great-niece, I adore,
I'm sixty-five she's not quite four,
Age doesn't matter as hand in hand,
We explore together God's wonderland.

CHRISTMAS ANGELS

Christmas angels prepared for their mission,
Watching carefully on Christmas Eve,
All the people who loved the Lord Jesus,
And the others who didn't believe.

In the mosques, synagogues, churches, chapels,
Angels smiled at the fervour they saw,
And they blessed the agnostics and seekers,
Who stood back but still knocked at the door.

In the street stood The Salvation Army,
Angels shared with the joy and the sound,
And they sang with the carols and music,
Joining in with the crowds standing round.

Then they went to The Meeting of Quakers,
Where the Friends sat in silence and prayer,
And they linked all the flames to the Godhead,
Spreading love and the light that was there.

Roman Catholics prayed with devotion,
Angels poured love on earnest, bowed heads,
And they calmed the excited, young children,
Who rushed prayers as they knelt by their beds.

They were there in the tropics and jungles,
Where our Christmas was something unknown,
And they scattered kindness and compassion,
As God's light shone as love seeds were sewn.

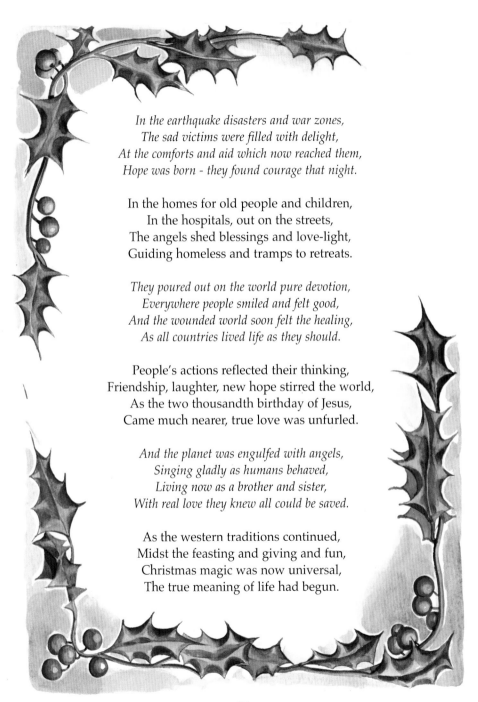

In the earthquake disasters and war zones,
The sad victims were filled with delight,
At the comforts and aid which now reached them,
Hope was born - they found courage that night.

In the homes for old people and children,
In the hospitals, out on the streets,
The angels shed blessings and love-light,
Guiding homeless and tramps to retreats.

They poured out on the world pure devotion,
Everywhere people smiled and felt good,
And the wounded world soon felt the healing,
As all countries lived life as they should.

People's actions reflected their thinking,
Friendship, laughter, new hope stirred the world,
As the two thousandth birthday of Jesus,
Came much nearer, true love was unfurled.

And the planet was engulfed with angels,
Singing gladly as humans behaved,
Living now as a brother and sister,
With real love they knew all could be saved.

As the western traditions continued,
Midst the feasting and giving and fun,
Christmas magic was now universal,
The true meaning of life had begun.

A FEW EXCERPTS FROM READERS LETTERS

"Something new has come into my life, your wonderful poetry! How can I thank you enough for all the enjoyment I had reading it. I had a dilemma- should I read one, savour it and leave the next one for tomorrow...You know the answer! I just couldn't I read the lot and then came back to select some again. A perfect bedside book, and do you know what? I am not into poetry AT ALL! ....I am too down to earth....but your poetry is truly wonderful and speaks straight to the heart! I had a great many laughs too! Bless you for sharing this great gift of yours with us all. I so look forward to reading your next book........"

Liliane Bell, Gerrards Cross, Bucks.

"An impression you have made when I was off work
A gap I had to fill,
Instead of lying in bed feeling so ill,
I popped into town, to the bookshop I went,
And what an investment on the £9.98 I spent.
I purchased your two books for the pretty bright covers,
And soon realised we're both poetry lovers.
I loved every one but what struck a cord,
Was the fact that you too are a child of the Lord.
So now I'm a fan I wait with anticipation,
My eyes are now peeled for your next publication.
You've really inspired me and so I had to tell,
Sent with love and blessings, Yours Rebecca Bell."
Rebecca Bell, Weymouth, Dorset.

"It was lovely to receive your beautiful little book of poems yesterday. I had a very enjoyable evening reading through such a wonderful selection, all so very different, but all so good! I love the way you are able to mix the humour in lot's as well!"

Barbara Stevens, Basingstoke, Hants

"Your introduction, which describes the book as 'sincere, simple poetry that comes direct from the heart' is a perfect description to which I would add the word beautiful. We do congratulate you, Chrissy, on this splendid production and pray that it will bring all you hope for into the lives of very many people.....I was wondering whether you would allow me to send this poem to some of the people who are looking for help?"

Brother Joseph. Bodmin, Cornwall.

"Thank you for your lovely book of poetry. I would like very much to buy it for myself as it is so inspiring and I can relate to so much of its sentiment. I particularly love the poem 'The Dress Fitting' as my own precious daughter Annette is to be married this August."

Catherine Combes, Fareham, Hants